Houghton Mifflin

Vocabulary Building and Dictionary Skills

Primary

Houghton Mifflin Company Boston

Atlanta Dallas Geneva, Illinois Lawrenceville, New Jersey Palo Alto Toronto

Contents

A, B, C Order	3
Looking Up a Word	7
Spelling a Word	8
The Things the Dictionary Tells Us About Words	9
Different Names for the Same Thing	14
Words That Name Opposite Things	15

Cover Photographs

Top left: **Dalmation** Robert Pearcy, Animals, Animals.
Top right: **apple** Fred Myers, Click/Chicago.
Bottom left: **heart** Petroff Photography.
Bottom right: **telephone** Sam Novak Photography, Ltd.

Illustrations: George Ulrich

Copyright ©1986 by Houghton Mifflin Company. All rights reserved. No part of this work may be reproduced or transmitted in any form or by any means, electronic or mechanical, including photocopying and recording, or by any information storage or retrieval system, except as may be expressly permitted by the 1976 Copyright Act or in writing by the Publisher.

Printed in the United States of America

ISBN 0-395-41396-6

NAME _____

ABC Order

A We use ABC order to find a word in the dictionary. Here is the alphabet. Some letters are not there. Put the right letter in each box. The first one is done for you.

ABC Order NAME _____

B Put the words in the balloons into ABC order. The first ones are done for you.

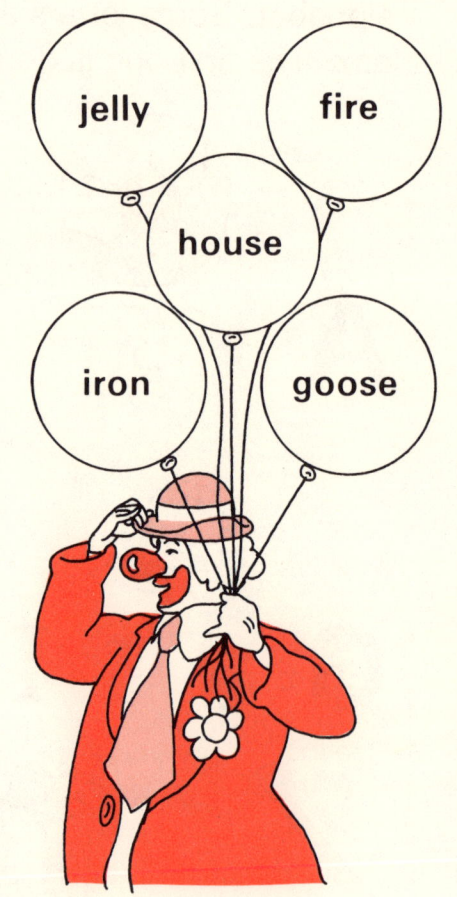

1. a l p h a b e t
2. _ _ _ _
3. _ _ _
4. _ _ _ _
5. _ _ _ _ _

1. f i r e
2. _ _ _ _ _
3. _ _ _ _ _
4. _ _ _ _
5. _ _ _ _ _

ABC Order NAME _____

1. k e y
2. ____
3. ___
4. ____
5. ____

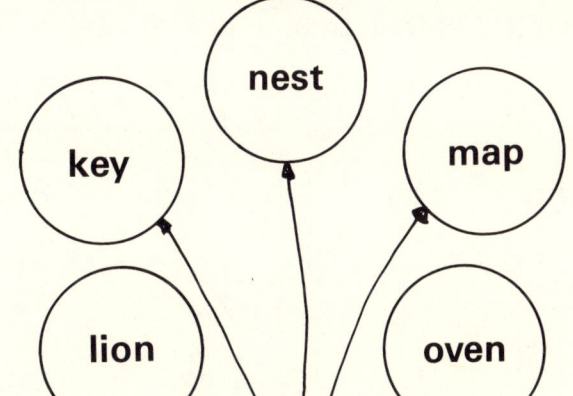

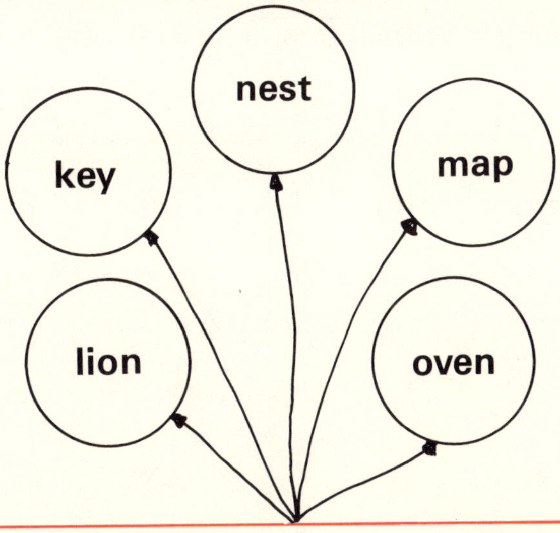

key, nest, map, lion, oven

1. p o n y
2. _____
3. ___
4. ____
5. _____

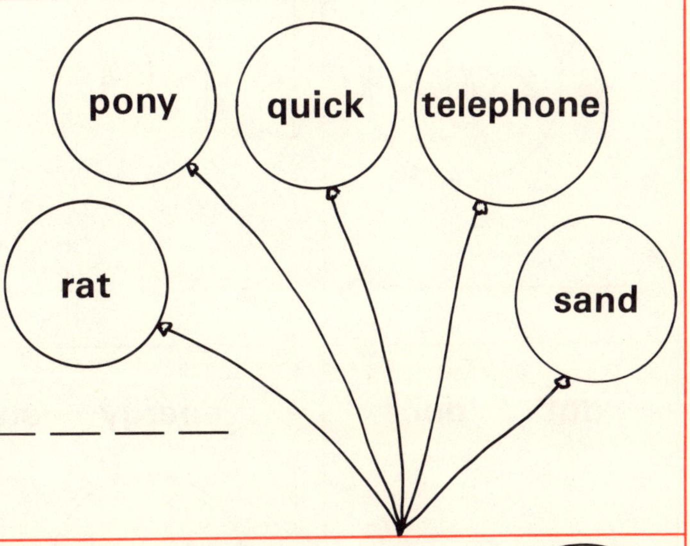

pony, quick, telephone, rat, sand

1. u m b r e l l a
2. _____
3. ____
4. ____
5. _____
6. ____

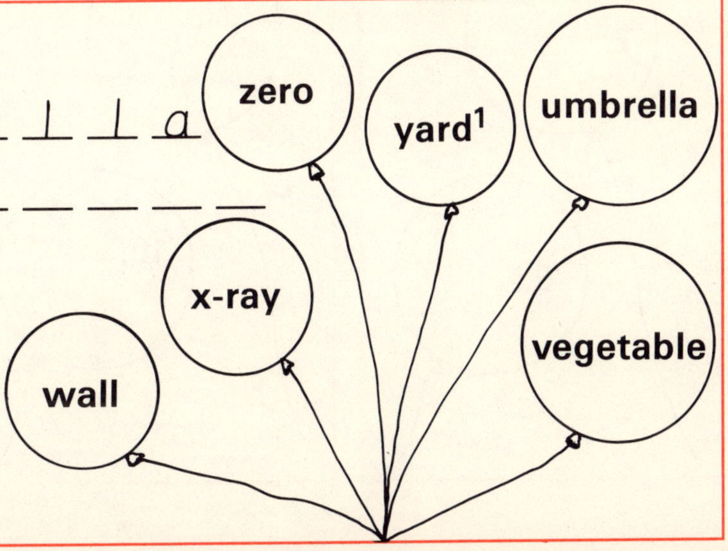

zero, yard[1], umbrella, x-ray, wall, vegetable

ABC Order

NAME _____

C Look at each pair of words. Put each pair of words into ABC order inside the balloons. The first one is done for you.

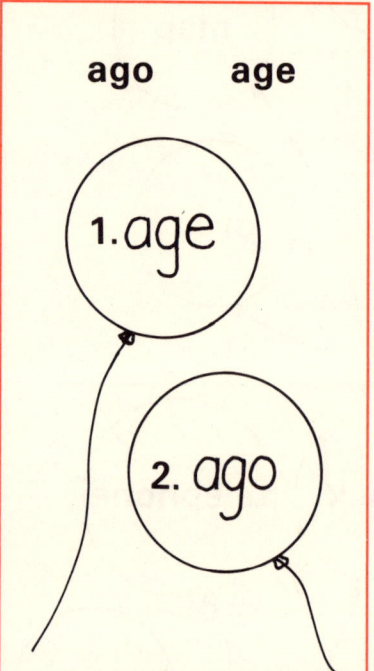

ago   age

1. age
2. ago

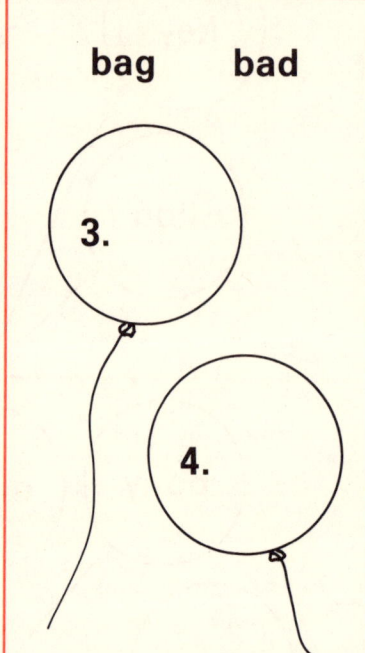

bag   bad

3.
4.

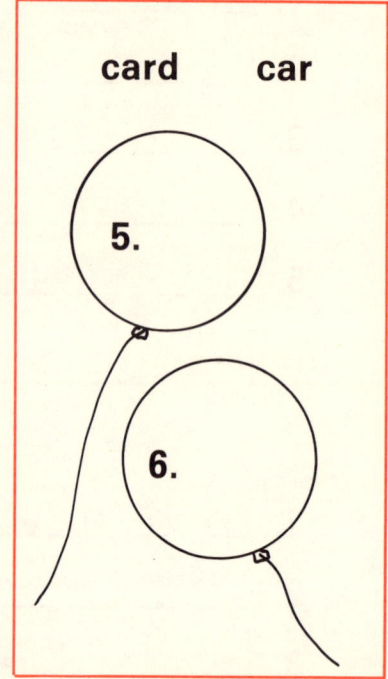

card   car

5.
6.

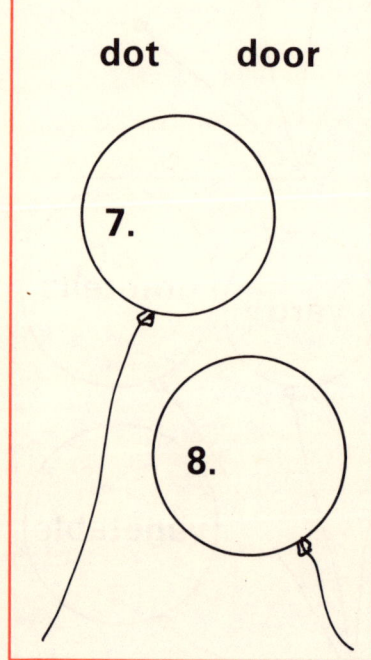

dot   door

7.
8.

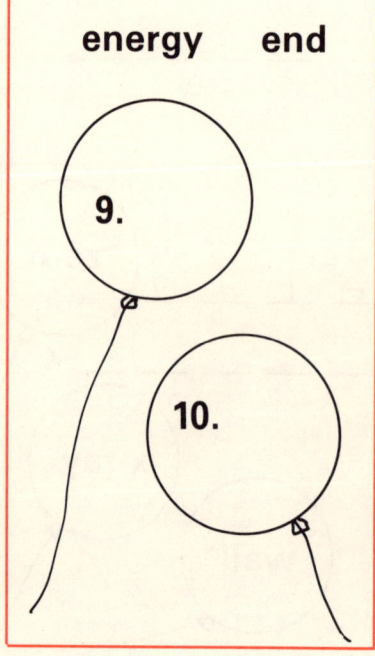

energy   end

9.
10.

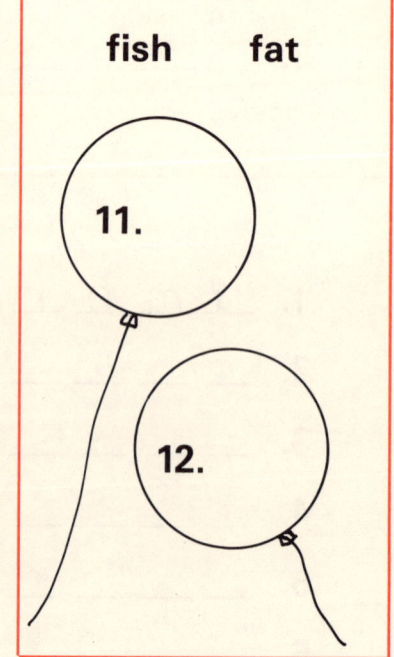

fish   fat

11.
12.

6

NAME _____

Looking Up a Word

These words are in your dictionary:

airplane	leaf
chimney	jump
bell	hen
engineer	rope
frog	map
deer	net

Look up each word. Write its page number in the empty space. The first one is done for you.

airplane page _4_

chimney page ____

bell page ____

engineer page ____

frog page ____

deer page ____

leaf page ____

jump page ____

hen page ____

rope page ____

map page ____

net page ____

Remember to use ABC order when you look up each word.

7

NAME _____

■ Spelling a Word

Look at each picture. What is the name of each thing? Spell the name of the thing you see. The first one is done for you.

1.    a n t

2.    b __ __ __

3.    c __ __

4.    d __ __ __

5.    f __ __ __

6.    m __ __ __ __ __ __

8

NAME _____

The Things the Dictionary Tells Us about Words

A These words are in your dictionary:

milk quickly
dinosaur because
heavy plant

Look up each word. Read what the dictionary tells you about each word. Read the sentences below. Use your dictionary to help you fill in the empty spaces. The first one is done for you.

1. **milk**

   Milk is a kind of liquid. It comes from <u>c o w s</u>, goats, and other animals. People drink <u>m i l k</u>. Parts of it are made into butter and <u>c h e e s e</u>.

2. **dinosaur**

   A **dinosaur** was a huge

   a _ _ _ _ _ _ .

   It lived millions of years ago. Some **dinosaurs** ate

   _ _ _ _ _ _

   and some of them ate other **dinosaurs**. Some **dinosaurs** grew to be as big as three

   _ _ _ _ _ _ _ _

   put together.

9

The Things the Dictionary Tells Us about Words

NAME _____

3. **heavy**

   Heavy objects are hard to l__ __ __ .

   Bowling balls are __ __ __ __ __ . Feathers are not.

4. **quickly**

   Lightning flashes in a moment. It flashes

   q__ __ __ __ __ __ .

5. **because**

   Elizabeth was hungry. So, she made a sandwich and ate it.

   She ate the sandwich b__ __ __ __ __ __ she was hungry.

6. **plant**

   A **plant** is anything alive that is not a person or an a__ __ __ __ __ .

   Most **plants** grow in the

   __ __ __ __ __ __ . Flowers, trees, and vegetables are all

   __ __ __ __ __ __ .

   Joe puts the pumpkin seeds in the ground.

   He p__ __ __ __ __ seeds every spring.

   The seeds he __ __ __ __ __ __ __ last spring grew into big pumpkins late in the fall.

10

The Things the Dictionary Tells Us about Words

NAME _____

B These words are in your dictionary:

1. car
2. firefighter
3. garden
4. hook
5. ladder
6. swan
7. triangle
8. xylophone

Look up each word. Read what the dictionary tells you about each word. Read the sentences below. Put a circle around YES if the sentence is right. Put a circle around NO if the sentence is wrong. The mouse did the first one for you.

1. **car**
   A **car** is a plant.   YES   (NO)

2. **firefighter**
   A **firefighter** is a person who puts out fires.   YES   NO

3. **garden**
   A **garden** is a building or part of a building.   YES   NO

4. **hook**
   A **hook** is a straight piece of metal.   YES   NO

5. **ladder**
   A **ladder** is used to climb up and down.   YES   NO

6. **swan**
   A **swan** is a small bird. It has a short neck.   YES   NO

7. **triangle**
   A **triangle** has four sides.   YES   NO

8. **xylophone**
   A **xylophone** is a kind of telephone.   YES   NO

The Things the Dictionary Tells Us about Words

NAME _____

C The dictionary often tells you more than one thing about a word. Numerals come before each new thing that the dictionary tells you about a word.

key

1. A **key** is a piece of metal. It opens a lock. Many people have **keys** to open the doors of their homes and cars.
2. A **key** is part of a piano. It is either white or black. When Peggy plays the piano, she puts her fingers on the **keys**.

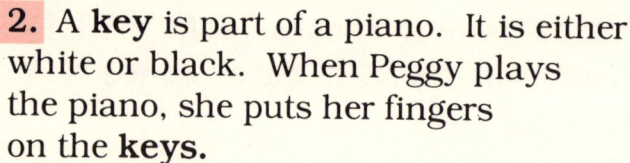

These words are in your dictionary:

key
trunk
needle

Look up each word. Read the things the dictionary tells you about each word. Use your dictionary to help you fill in the empty spaces. The first one is done for you.

key

1. A **key** is a piece of m e t a l . It opens a l o c k . Many people have **keys** to open the doors of their homes and cars.

2. A **key** is part of a __ __ __ __ __ . It is either __ __ __ __ __ or __ __ __ __ __ . When Peggy plays the piano, she puts her fingers on the **keys**.

12

The Things the Dictionary Tells Us about Words

NAME _____

trunk

1. The **trunk** is the thick part of a t __ __ __ . It grows up the middle of the tree. Branches grow out of **trunks**.

2. A **trunk** is a large __ __ __ . Larry takes a **trunk** filled with clothes to camp.

3. A **trunk** is part of an __ __ __ __ __ __ __ __ .

   It looks like a very long __ __ __ __ . An elephant can pick up things with its **trunk**.

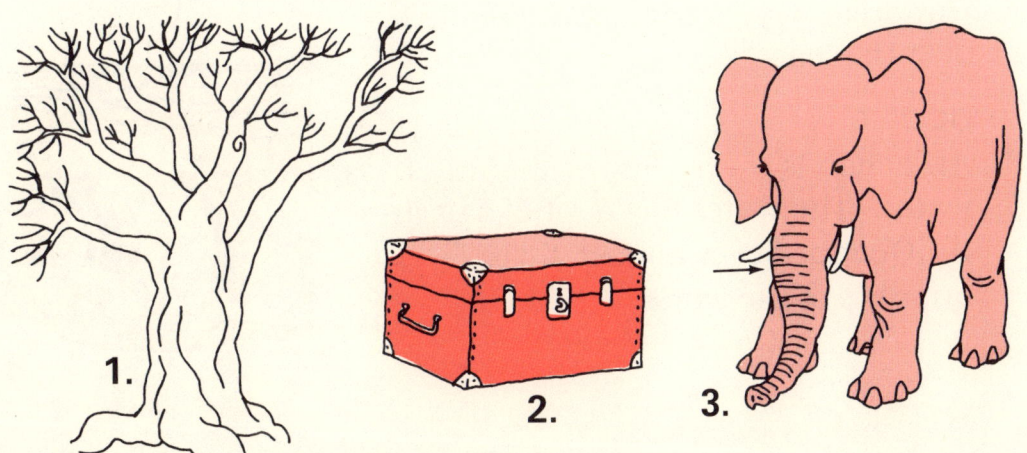

1.   2.   3.

needle

1. A **needle** is a kind of t __ __ __ . It is a short and very thin piece of __ __ __ __ __ . **Needles** have holes at one end and sharp points at the other. People use **needles** and thread to __ __ __ clothes.

2. A **needle** is a kind of __ __ __ __ . It is shaped like the **needle** people use to sew with. This **needle** is found on __ __ __ __ trees.

13

NAME _____

Different Names for the Same Thing

Sometimes we use different names for the same thing. The dictionary tells you different words for the same thing. *Sea* and *ocean* are big amounts of water.

sea
Sea is another name for **ocean**. Hundreds of years ago pirates sailed over the seas.

ocean
An **ocean** is a very large amount of water. The water has a lot of salt in it. **Oceans** cover almost three quarters of the world.

Look up each word in List A. Read what the dictionary tells you about each word. Put a circle around the word in List B that is another name for the word across from it in List A. The first one is done for you.

LIST A	LIST B
1. **sea**	1. lake pond (ocean)
2. **someone**	2. somebody something sometimes
3. **automobile**	3. train tractor car
4. **gift**	4. present[1] loan birthday
5. **autumn**	5. summer fall[1] winter
6. **phone**	6. telescope phonograph telephone

14

NAME _____

■ Words That Name Opposite Things

Some words name opposite things. The dictionary tells you about them. *Fast* is the opposite of *slow*. See what the dictionary tells you about *fast* and *slow*.

fast
Fast is the opposite of slow. Rabbits move quickly. They are **fast** animals. Turtles are not **fast**.

slow
Slow is the opposite of fast. A lot of time passes while turtles move. Turtles are **slow** animals.

Words That Name Opposite Things   NAME _____

Do this puzzle. Find the opposite of each word in the list. Find the arrow with the numeral for each word. Fill in the boxes after the arrow with the opposite of the word in the list. Look at the words in the stars for more help. The first two are done for you.

1. slow
2. many
3. top
4. weak
5. day
6. dry
7. old
8. back
9. rough
10. big
11. on
12. wild
13. less
14. above
15. close
16. light[1]
17. no